Mighty Machines
TRACTORS
AND FARM VEHICLES

Jean Coppendale

QEB Publishing

First published in the United States by
QEB Publishing, Inc.
3 Wrigley, Suite A
Irvine, CA 92618

www.qed-publishing.co.uk

Written by Jean Coppendale
Designed by Joita Das (Q2A Media)
Editor Katie Bainbridge
Picture Researcher Jyoti Sachdev (Q2A Media)

ISBN 978 1 60992 360 0

Printed in China

Picture credits

Key: t = top, b = bottom, c = centre,
l = left, r = right, FC = front cover
CLAAS KGaA ltd: 5t; Dave Reede/**AGStockUSA:** 6-7;
Mirek Weichsel/**AGStockUSA:** 10-11;
Index Stock Imagery/ Photolibrary: 10b;
Agripictures: 13t; Dave Reede/**AGStockUSA:** 14-15;
Holt Studios: 15t; **CLAAS:** 16-17;
New Holland: 18-19; **Valtra:** 20-21

Words in **bold** can be found
in the glossary on page 23.

Contents

What is a tractor? 4

Watch those wheels! 6

Preparing the fields 8

Sowing the seeds 10

Taking care of the crops 12

Harvest time 14

Collecting wheat 16

Baling hay 18

Pull, tractor! 20

Activities 22

Glossary 23

Index 24

What is a **tractor?**

cab

The cab has large windows so the driver can see what is happening.

This tractor is pulling a heavy trailer across a field.

Tractors are big machines that are used mostly on farms. They help farmers prepare their land and plant, care for and **harvest** their crops.

A tractor has a **cab**. The driver sits in the cab. Other machines can be hooked onto the back of a tractor, so it can do many different jobs.

Watch those wheels!

9390

A tractor has big wheels, so it can travel across bumpy fields. The huge wheels also help stop the tractor from sinking into mud.

Some tractors have two or even three sets of wheels on each side.

Tractor wheels are made to grip soft, muddy ground.

Preparing the fields

Farmers need to prepare their fields before they can plant **crops**. To do this, farmers attache a **plow** to the back of the tractor.

A plow is a long row of metal blades. The blades are pulled through the earth.

The plow has sharp **blades** that cut through the dirt. The tractor pulls the plow through the fields. The blades break up the dirt and turn it over. The plow makes rows of ditches, or **furrows**.

Sowing the seeds

When the fields are prepared, farmers plant,
or sow, seeds. They do this with a seed drill.
A seed drill is a container, or row of containers,
that is attached to the back of a tractor.
The containers are filled with seeds.

This seed drill is being
filled with corn seeds.

As the seed drill is pulled across the fields by the tractor, seeds are dropped into the furrows in the ground.

The seed drill plants the seeds in straight rows.

Taking care of the crops

Once they start growing, the new crops need to be cared for. Some farmers spray their crops with a special liquid. The liquid stops bugs from eating the plants. The liquid also stops weeds from growing.

Some farmers do not spray their crops. Instead, workers remove weeds with their hands as they are pulled through the fields.

A machine called a crop sprayer can be hooked to the back of a tractor. As the tractor moves through the fields, liquid is sprayed on the growing crops.

A crop sprayer has long arms on each side. The liquid sprays out of these arms.

Harvest time

When crops are fully grown, they must be harvested. Different machines are used to harvest different crops. Vegetable harvesters dig up vegetables that grow under the ground.

The green tractor is pulling a machine that harvests potatoes.

Vegetable harvesters pull vegetables out of the ground. Then the vegetables are dropped into a truck.

Some harvesters can dig up two rows of carrots at a time.

Collecting wheat

Wheat is ready to harvest when it is tall and **ripe**. This is done with a machine called a combine harvester. The front of a combine harvester has sharp blades.

Many combine harvesters work together to harvest large fields.

As the blades of a combine harvester move, they cut the long stalks of wheat.

The wheat is sucked into the harvester. The **grain** of the wheat is separated from its stalk inside the harvester.

Baling straw

After a field of wheat has been harvested, the cut stalks are left behind. This is called straw. A special machine called a baler gathers the straw and makes it into round or square **bales**.

The bales of straw are tied up tightly and dropped out of the baler.

New Holland

BR560

A tractor loads bales of straw onto a trailer. The bales are then taken away to be stored.

The straw is used as bedding for farm animals. It helps to keep them warm, especially in the winter.

Pull, tractor!

Some tractors can be used for work—and for play! Tractor pulls are very exciting. People watch tractor pulls to see which tractor will pull the heaviest load.

20

The tractors race on a special **track**. They have huge back wheels to stop them from slipping. The tractors pull a heavy load behind them while the crowd cheers.

During a pull, a tractor's front wheels may lift off the ground.

Activities

- Would you like to be a farmer who drives a big tractor? Would it be fun? Would it be hard work? Draw a picture of yourself driving a tractor.

- Here are two tractors you have seen in this book. Can you remember what jobs they do?

- Write a story about a runaway tractor. How will your story start? Who will be in your story? What happens at the end? Can you draw a picture to go with your story?

- Look through the book again. Write a list of jobs that are done on the farm and the machines you need to do them. How many different machines are needed? Which job do you think would be your favorite? Why?

Glossary

Bales
Large bundles of cut hay that are tied up very tightly.

Blades
Sharp, flat pieces of metal used for cutting.

Cab
The place where the tractor driver sits and uses the controls to move the tractor.

Crops
Plants that farmers grow, such as vegetables or wheat.

Furrows
Long, narrow cuts in the ground made by a plow.

Grain
The part of the wheat that is used to make flour for bread. Grains are like tiny seeds.

Harvest
To cut and collect all the crops that are fully grown or ripe.

Plow
A machine that breaks up the dirt and prepares it for seeds to be planted.

Ripe
Crops that are fully grown and ready to harvest.

Track
A special path where tractors race.

Index

activities 22

animals 19

baler 18

bales 18, 23

baling hay 18–19

blades 8, 9, 16, 17, 23

bugs 12

cab 4, 5, 23

carrot harvester 15

combine harvester 16–17

crop sprayer 13

crops 5, 8, 12–13, 23

driver 4, 5

farms 5, 23

fields 8–9

furrows 9, 11, 23

grain 17, 23

harvest 5, 14–17, 23

hay 18–19

plow 8–9, 23

potato harvester 14–15

preparing fields 5, 8–9

pulling weights 20–21

races 20–21

ripe 16, 23

seed drill 10–11

sowing seeds 10–11

sprays 12, 13

track 21, 23

tractor pulls 20–21

trailers 5

vegetable harvesters 14–15

weeds 12, 13

wheat 16–17, 18

wheels 6–7, 21